NATURE IN THE NEWS

THE PAKISTAN EARTHQUAKE

Colleen Adams

PowerKiDS press™

J551.22
ADA

New York

Published in 2007 by The Rosen Publishing Group, Inc.
29 East 21st Street, New York, NY 10010

Copyright © 2007 by The Rosen Publishing Group, Inc.

Book Design: Dan Hosek

ISBN-13: 978-1-4042-3539-6
ISBN-10: 1-4042-3539-6

Manufactured in the United States of America

CONTENTS

DANGER IN THE MOUNTAINS

At 8:50 a.m. on October 8, 2005, a large earthquake rocked an area in the **Himalayas** known as Kashmir. The quake measured 7.6 on the **moment magnitude scale**. Many villages and even some cities were completely destroyed by the earthquake, leaving millions without shelter. Many of the buildings in this area were made of simple materials, such as wood and clay bricks. As a result, thousands of structures—including countless schools and hospitals—were ruined in seconds. Thousands of people lost their lives. Numerous landslides and a harsh Himalayan winter made conditions even worse.

This was one of the deadliest earthquakes in recorded history. More than 74,000 people lost their lives, and about 3.3 million people were left homeless.

Muzaffarabad, Pakistan

AFGHANISTAN

Kabul

PAKISTAN-CONTROLLED KASHMIR

CHINA

Muzaffarabad

Islamabad

INDIAN-CONTROLLED KASHMIR

PAKISTAN

INDIA

5

WHAT IS AN EARTHQUAKE?

Earth's crust is made up of many slowly moving **tectonic plates**. On average, the plates are about 60 miles (97 km) thick and "float" on the soft, hot rock of the **mantle**. As the plates move very slowly, pressure builds between them and they may bend. After a long time, these plates can move suddenly, releasing the pressure and causing the ground to shake.

When the plates suddenly move and snap into a new position, they release **seismic waves**. These waves grow weaker the farther away they travel from the **epicenter** of the quake. Smaller earthquakes called aftershocks commonly follow larger quakes. Aftershocks are a result of the plate or plates settling into new positions.

Tectonic plates move only a few inches (cm) every year. ▶

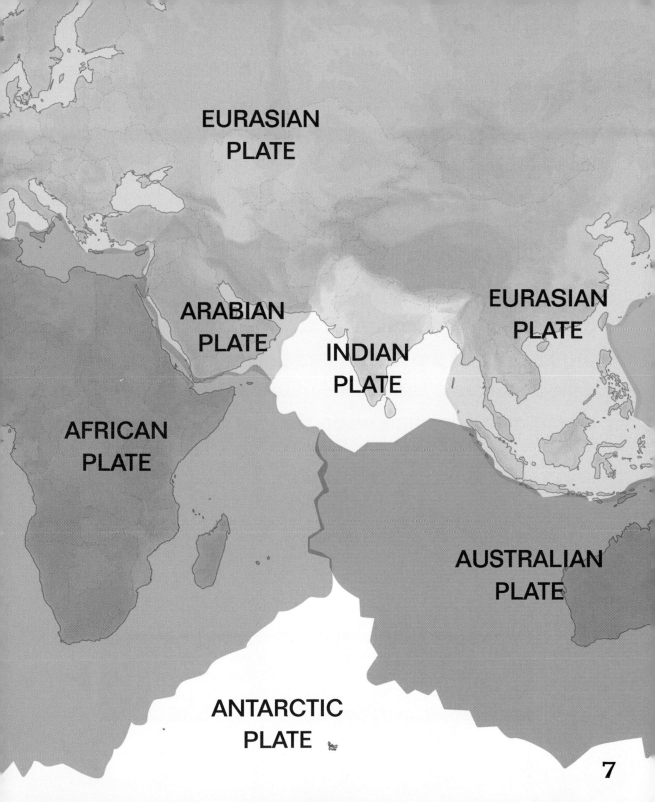

EURASIAN PLATE

EURASIAN PLATE

ARABIAN PLATE

INDIAN PLATE

AFRICAN PLATE

AUSTRALIAN PLATE

ANTARCTIC PLATE

An earthquake can cause widespread damage. Buildings and other structures may **collapse**, with costly and deadly results. People may be trapped or killed inside them.

Earthquakes are very often followed by fires due to broken gas and electric lines. Broken water lines make it difficult or impossible to fight fire. Landslides can block escape and rescue routes, and can also bury entire communities. Earthquakes that occur at the bottom of the ocean can cause giant waves called tsunamis (soo-NAH-mees). These waves can cause great damage when they hit land.

The most destructive earthquake to hit the United States occurred in San Francisco, California, in 1906. The quake destroyed about 28,000 buildings and started many fires that burned for days.

9

JAMMU AND KASHMIR

Jammu and Kashmir—usually shortened to Kashmir—is a mountainous region on the border between India and Pakistan. Both countries claim to own the region, and neither will recognize the other's claim. A large part of the region is governed by the Indian government, and another is governed by the Pakistani government. China also claims to own a small portion of Kashmir.

Between these regions is a border known as the "Line of Control." For the past 60 years, fighting has frequently broken out between India and Pakistan near this line. To this day, the Kashmir region remains a source of conflict between the two countries.

Jammu and Kashmir was once an independent country. The name Kashmir comes from the name of a beautiful valley in this region. ▶

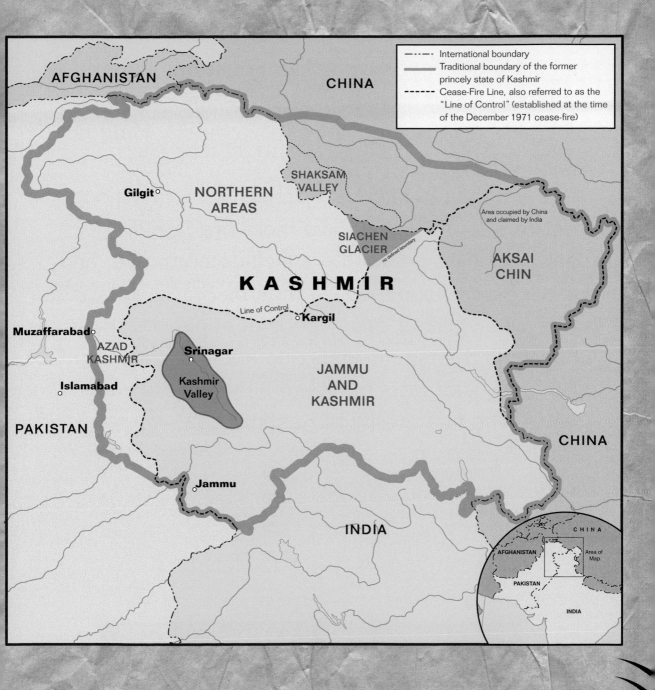

AFGHANISTAN

CHINA

Gilgit

NORTHERN
AREAS

SHAKSAM
VALLEY

Area occupied by China
and claimed by India

SIACHEN
GLACIER

no defined boundary

AKSAI
CHIN

K A S H M I R

Line of Control

Kargil

Muzaffarabad

AZAD
KASHMIR

Srinagar

Kashmir
Valley

JAMMU
AND
KASHMIR

Islamabad

CHINA

PAKISTAN

Jammu

INDIA

CHINA

AFGHANISTAN

Area of
Map

PAKISTAN

INDIA

11

The people of Kashmir come from different backgrounds, each with its own customs and traditions. More than 70 percent of the people of Kashmir are **Muslim**. The rest are mostly **Hindus** and **Buddhists**.

Even though most of Kashmir is mountainous, most of the people who live there are farmers. Common crops grown there include corn, rice, and wheat. Some people have orchards that grow apples, pears, and walnuts. Many people, especially those who live in the mountains, raise sheep, goats, and yaks. They use wool to create beautiful rugs and shawls. The fine quality of Kashmir goat wool— commonly known as cashmere—is valued all over the world.

About 13 million people live in Jammu and Kashmir. The peace-loving people of this region would like to be an independent country again.

13

The region of Kashmir has always had seismic activity. The Himalaya mountain range was formed by the meeting of two tectonic plates. Millions of years ago, the Indian Plate began moving north. It met the Eurasian Plate and kept moving north, causing the land to pile up between the plates. As the India Plate continues to push against the Eurasian Plate, the mountains continue to grow higher. This movement causes frequent earthquakes.

Records of earthquakes in Kashmir go back more than 1,000 years. They show that the 1500s were a particularly active time for earthquakes.

In 1974, the Pattan earthquake struck Kashmir. Although it destroyed several villages and killed about 5,000 people, this quake was not as destructive as the quake of 2005 because it hit an area where few people lived.

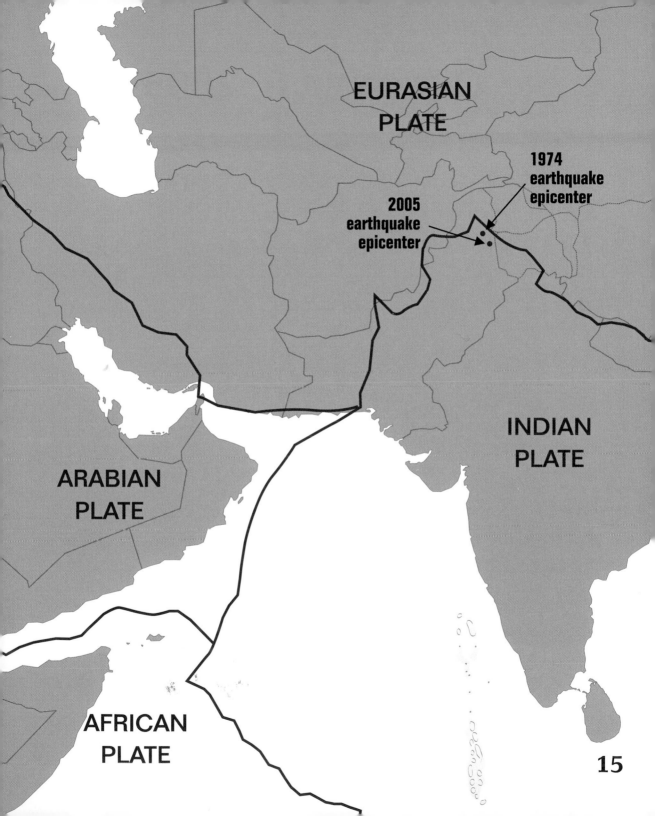

EURASIAN
PLATE

1974
earthquake
epicenter

2005
earthquake
epicenter

INDIAN
PLATE

ARABIAN
PLATE

AFRICAN
PLATE

15

October 8, 2005

The Pakistan earthquake struck on a Saturday at 8:50 a.m. At this time, most young children were at school, and many people were at work. The quake was so sudden and powerful that many people did not have time to escape from buildings before the structures fell on them.

Although deaths and property damage were reported in the India-governed section of Kashmir and in Afghanistan, the destruction in the section of Kashmir governed by Pakistan was much worse. The epicenter of the quake was about 12 miles (19 km) north-northeast of the city of Muzaffarabad in the Pakistani region called Azad Kashmir.

The quake flattened a ten-story apartment building 62 miles (100 km) away from the epicenter in the Pakistani capital of Islamabad.

Since northern Pakistan and northern India are located in one of the most mountainous regions in the world, the quake caused hundreds of deadly landslides. Homes, farmland, and entire villages were covered with earth and rock in just a few seconds. Landslides claimed many lives and caused many injuries.

The landslides also broke important lines of communication. Power lines and telephone lines snapped, making it very difficult for **survivors** to call for help. Most of the roads became blocked as well. This stopped survivors from escaping the **disaster** area quickly. It also kept rescue workers from reaching the people who needed them most.

Here, Pakistani soldiers examine a road in Nauseri, Pakistan, that was buried by a landslide caused by the quake. ▶

AFTER THE QUAKE

In the days after the earthquake, dozens of aftershocks continued to shake Kashmir. One measured 6.3 on the **Richter scale**. These constant rumblings kept the survivors afraid for their lives.

So many buildings had collapsed during the earthquake that about 3.3 million people were believed to have been left homeless. Many of the buildings were schools. Some relief organizations such as the Red Cross believe that one-third of the people who died in the quake were children. Hundreds of hospitals were also destroyed, which made treating injured survivors even more difficult.

The city of Balakot was home to about 30,000 people. Built on two major fault lines (the border where two tectonic plates meet), the city was almost completely destroyed during the quake. The Pakistani government has said that Balakot will be rebuilt in a new and safer location.

21

In the days following the quake, the numerous landslides proved to be the worst continuing effect of the disaster. Authorities from India and Pakistan allowed five crossing points to be opened on the Line of Control so relief could be delivered more quickly.

Some landslides blocked valleys, creating natural dams and temporary lakes. Scientists think that these natural dams are not strong enough to hold back the water. They could break and flood the surrounding areas. Some mountain slopes that did not break and crumble were left cracked and unstable. The danger of more landslides occurring remains a serious problem.

The first rescuers to reach some survivors high in the mountains arrived on foot, carrying supplies on mules. Others arrived by helicopter.

SURVIVING WINTER

After the quake, millions of people were left without a place to live. Many were dressed in rags and slept under pieces of wood propped against rocks or out in the open. Many didn't even want to be inside buildings, fearing that another quake would strike. As the snow started to fall, survivors and rescuers began to worry that many more people would die in the freezing Himalayan winter.

Many survivors began the long walk to camps being set up in the hills and valleys. Some had to walk hundreds of miles (km) to reach these camps. Others refused to leave the land where their families had lived for many years.

The mountainous regions of Kashmir receive heavy snowfall in the winter season, which lasts from November to May. During this time, travel is very difficult or impossible because of deep snow.

Camps with rows and rows of tents were set up for the survivors. Relief workers organized the camps and provided food, shelter, and health care for the survivors. The food and shelter supplied by these camps were just enough to help survivors make it through the winter months. Relief workers tried to set up schools for the children living in the camps, but they lacked space, trained teachers, and learning materials. The camps filled up quickly and soon became overcrowded. Most of the camps became cities of tents housing thousands of families.

These survivors are living in a camp in Kashtra, Pakistan. In November 2005, about 2,600 people were living there.

REBUILDING LIVES

On March 31, 2006, the Pakistani government turned off the electricity and water in the camps. They feared the camps would become permanent settlements where survivors would depend on the aid they received. Survivors who had been living in the camps were forced to return to their communities in the mountains—and most of those communities were just piles of rubble. Many survivors had to take the tents they had lived in for the past 4 months with them, because their homes had been destroyed. The children who survived started going back to school in tents. Few communities had electricity or running water.

Like many survivors, this family in Batian, Pakistan, had very little to return to after the camp they had been living in closed.

29

Collapsed buildings and numerous landslides made it very difficult for rescuers and builders to reach the mountain communities that had been hit hardest by the quake. Even after 6 months, many villages looked the same as they had just seconds after the earthquake struck. Many survivors did not have homes to return to. Millions of dollars are still needed to help rebuild the communities that were destroyed by the quake.

People from around the world are working very hard to help the people of Kashmir. Their work, however, has just begun. Many think it will be a long time before this area of the world returns to life as it was before the earthquake.

GLOSSARY

Buddhist (BOO-dihst) Someone who practices the religion of Buddhism.

collapse (kuh-LAPS) To fall apart suddenly.

disaster (dih-ZAS-tuhr) An event that causes widespread damage, death, and hardship.

epicenter (EH-pih-sehn-tuhr) The exact location on Earth's surface directly above the spot where an earthquake starts.

Himalayas (hih-muh-LAY-uhz) A mountain system in Asia that includes the tallest mountains in the world.

Hindu (HIHN-doo) Someone who practices the religion of Hinduism.

mantle (MAN-tuhl) The layer of Earth below the crust and above the core.

moment magnitude scale (MOH-muhnt MAG-nuh-tood SKAYL) A scale used to measure the energy released by an earthquake. It was introduced in 1979 and is used instead of the Richter scale for very large earthquakes.

Muslim (MUHZ-luhm) Someone who practices the religion of Islam.

Richter scale (RIHK-tuhr SKAYL) A scale used to measure the energy released by an earthquake.

seismic wave (SYZ-mihk WAYV) A wave caused by an earthquake that travels through Earth.

survivor (suhr-VY-vuhr) Someone who lives through a terrible event.

tectonic plate (tehk-TAH-nihk PLAYT) One of the many sections of Earth's crust that float on a layer of hot, soft rock.

INDEX

WEB SITES

Due to the changing nature of Internet links, PowerKids Press has developed an online list of Web sites related to the subject of this book. This site is updated regularly. Please use this link to access the list:
http://www.powerkidslinks.com/natnews/pakearth/